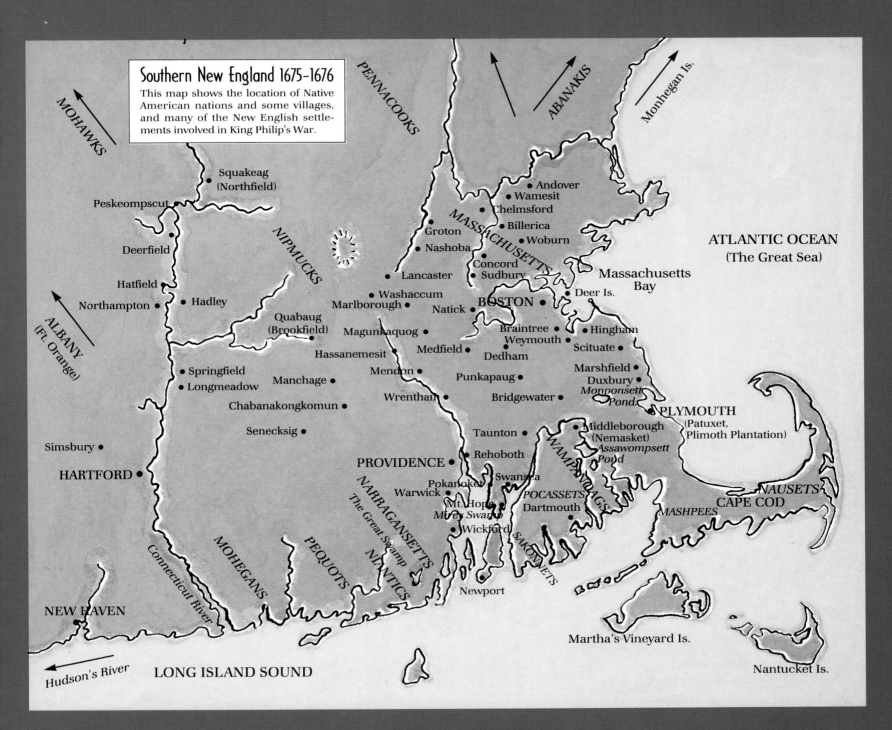

Southern New England 1675-1676

This map shows the location of Native American nations and some villages, and many of the New English settlements involved in King Philip's War.

MOHAWKS

PENNACOOKS

ABANAKIS

Monhegan Is.

Squakeag
(Northfield)

Peskeompscut

Deerfield

Hatfield

Northampton

Hadley

ALBANY
(Ft. Orange)

NIPMUCKS

Quabaug
(Brookfield)

Groton

Nashoba

Lancaster

Washaccum

Marlborough

Andover

Wamesit

Chelmsford

Billerica

Woburn

MASSACHUSETTS

Concord

Sudbury

Natick

BOSTON

Deer Is.

Massachusetts
Bay

ATLANTIC OCEAN
(The Great Sea)

Magunkaquog

Hassanemesit

Springfield

Longmeadow

Manchage

Mendon

Medfield

Braintree

Weymouth

Dedham

Hingham

Scituate

Chabanakongkomun

Wrentham

Punkapaug

Bridgewater

Marshfield

Duxbury

Monponsett
Pond

Taunton

Middleborough
(Nemasket)

Assawompsett
Pond

PLYMOUTH
(Patuxet,
Plimoth Plantation)

Senecksig

Simsbury

HARTFORD

PROVIDENCE

Rehoboth

Swansea

Pokanoket

Warwick

NARRAGANSETTS

The Great Swamp

Mt. Hope

Mirey Swamp

Wickford

PEQUOTS

NIANTICS

Connecticut River

MOHEGANS

NEW HAVEN

Newport

Hudson's River

LONG ISLAND SOUND

POCASSETS

Dartmouth

WAMPANOAGS

SAKONNETS

MASHPEES

CAPE COD

NAUSETS

Martha's Vineyard Is.

Nantucket Is.

THUNDER FROM THE CLEAR SKY

WRITTEN AND ILLUSTRATED BY MARCIA SEWALL

ALADDIN PAPERBACKS
New York London Toronto Sydney New Delhi

ACKNOWLEDGEMENTS

I wish to thank William M. Fowler, Jr., president of the New England Historic Genealogical Society and editor of the *New England Quarterly,* for reading my manuscript; and John Peters (Slow Turtle), Commissioner of Indian Affairs for the state of Massachusetts, and supreme medicine man for the Wampanoag Nation, for reading the manuscript and checking the illustrations for details of Wampanoag life.

Information on Wampanoag customs and beliefs comes from *New England's Prospect* by William Wood (pp. 95-96), and *The Spirit of New England Tribes* by William S. Simmons (p. 71), which also provided the book's title (p. 84).

Material on page 18 was quoted from Increase Mather; on page 29, from Thomas Morton and Robert Cushman; on page 36, from Increase Mather.

The map (endpapers) was adapted from one by D. E. Leach that appeared in *Flintlock and Tomahawk.*

Regarding the page 41 illustration: Because the rope broke, Tobias's son survived the hanging, but he was executed shortly thereafter.

Great Spirit, grant that I may not criticize my neighbor
until I have walked a mile in his moccasins.
—*NATIVE AMERICAN PRAYER*

Boast not proud English of thy birth and blood,
Thy brother Indian is by birth as Good.
—*ROGER WILLIAMS*

A Wampanoag's Story

Pokanoket, Towwa'keeswosh Moon (When the women hill the corn) 1675

Strange white folk one day shall come across the Great Sea and crowd red men off the earth—so an old sachem warned our people many, many winters ago.

Then, one day when my grandfather's grandfather was a young man, across the Great Sea floated an island with tall trees upon it, hung with white clouds. My ancestor and his friends paddled their mishoons toward it thinking they might pick strawberries there, but as they neared, claps of thunder sounded from the clear sky. Deep my ancient people thrust their paddles into the sea and glided to safety. Soon, laughing, pale-faced men could be seen around the edge of the island, coat-wearers with strange beards, calling out words not of our tongue. They beckoned to my grandfather's grandfather and his friends to come to them and so they found the island to be like a great mishoon with squares of cloth hung in its branchless trees. Thunder from their shooting sticks pierced the sky.

My people thought the white ones had come searching for firewood, but the coat-wearers laughed, held up fish, and pointed to the sea. Soon, my ancestor and his friends paddled back to shore, each with a string of sunlit beads, a gift from the pale-faced men. This story my grandmother often told me.

For many moons since that day long ago, my people have watched boats filled with white folk sail the coast here.

We liked their pretty trinkets and iron kettles, their metal tools and trucking cloth . . . and their shooting sticks. They especially liked our animal skins, our corn seed, and wampum beads. Wampum, sacred to our people, was like money to the traders and was exchanged by them up and down the coast for whatever they desired.

We trapped many, many of our beaver friends and traded their furs to the white ones for their treasures until beavers became scarce. Then we watched as Englishmen's ships, loaded with wood from our forest, disappeared over the Great Sea. Deer that once browsed at the edges of our sunny fields now retreated into the forest as the English cleared land and hunted, too.

It seemed as though our slowly turning circle of days and moons and winters had become shapeless. It seemed as though the once firm earth we walked upon trembled beneath our footsteps as our paths crossed with those of white men.

Then there was terrible sickness about. Soon after white folk were first seen upon our shores, diseases spread through our villages. The years 1616–1617, by the white man's calendar, were death-filled. We watched helplessly as medicine men tried to free the bad spirits from our dying loved ones. We were so desperately sick we hadn't even the strength to bury our dead. What had we done to displease Kiehtan? Were these illnesses given to our people by the white man's God? Could he possibly be more powerful than our Great Spirit?

Bad feelings had existed between white men and red men since pale-faced coat-wearers first came to our shores. Like blood through water, word spread among all the different nations living at the edge of the Great Sea that white folk could not be trusted. Up the coast where the waters of the Great Sea are cold, white men invited native people on board their ships and captured them. We knew this was so for Squanto and a group of his friends were enticed on board an Englishman's vessel, held fast against their will, and stolen away to be sold as slaves.

After a handful of winters had passed, Squanto managed to safely return home. Finding his village of Patuxet made empty by death, he went to live in a village nearby. During the first moon of winter a ship filled with English families arrived off the Patuxet shore. The year was 1620 by the white man's calendar. We who lived not far away wondered at their intent. It seemed so strange that among them were women and children, for none had come here before on white men's ships. Hiding nearby, we watched their struggle to survive.

On that vessel were people whom we now call Pilgrims, and our empty village of Patuxet was soon named Plimoth Plantation by them.

Well hidden in a dark swamp, our medicine men gathered to speak of their visions regarding this settlement of newcomers. Guided by their wisdom, our sachems then made their thoughts known among our people. Massasoit said it was wise to be friends with the English, for we had needs. Corbitant warned that more white ones would arrive if these were not driven back into the sea. At last, a decision for peace was made.

Samoset, a sagamore visiting from Monhegan Island, approached the Pilgrims. Speaking in their own tongue he said, "Welcome, welcome Englishmen." Within a handful of days Squanto, then Chief Massasoit, arrived with greetings for the Pilgrims. He and their chief, John Carver, saw fit to bind our nation and the Pilgrim settlement together in an agreement of trust and friendship. We promised to give them protection against anyone causing war with them and they promised to give us the same. It pleased us in our weakened state, for now Englishmen's muskets could be turned against our enemy, the Narragansetts. That Massasoit agreed to have our people tried and punished by Englishmen and English laws was not good, for we were not permitted to do the same. That Massasoit later agreed that we should trade our animal skins only with Plymouth Colony and that we should trade lands only with their consent was not good, for it gave the white ones power over us. Our great sachem made these decisions for he thought they were best for us. He loved his people, but we, once so independent, found our backs now bent in submission.

A double handful of summers after the settlement of Plimoth Plantation a new colony, Massachusetts Bay, was formed a half day's run up the coast. As Corbitant had predicted, no sooner did one ship arrive than more followed. Within a few years English people swarmed over this land. They said they had come to form a godly community and wished to turn us natives into praying folk like themselves. Little did they try to understand our Spirit World!

When beavers became scarce, then beaver skins were no longer plentiful for trade; when silver coins became available here and wampum was no longer needed as money, then we had only land for exchange. For some cloth, hatchets, hoes, and perhaps a musket or two, we gave the Englishmen land from the river to the sea, to the faraway hill and back again. It seemed a fair trade. Although a piece of parchment with the seal of a distant king and the marks of our leaders said the land now belonged to the English, we knew the land was sacred and was to be shared by all. We thought we could still hunt in the woods and fish in the lakes and streams. But the English put up fences, mapped out boundaries, and pointed to treaties written in a tongue we did not fully understand.

Dealings among the Wampanoags and Narragansetts, Pequots, Niantics and Mohegans, Nipmucks, Massachusetts and Pennacooks, Abanakis and Mohawks always have risen and sunk like a pot of boiling samp. Now there are English settlements at Boston, Plymouth, Hartford, Newport, and Providence; and the Dutch at Hudson's River and Albany, and the French up where the cold winds come from, have become a part of this ever-thickening porridge. Friends become enemies and enemies become friends depending upon events and desires and needs. There are traitors among us and we fear their treachery.

As long as Chief Massasoit lived, our Wampanoag people remained at peace with the English. But we could not forget how men from Plimoth Plantation deceived and murdered warriors of the Massachusetts nation living nearby.

Red men and white men are infected with suspicion for one another. How much we desire Englishmen's muskets! Anyone's muskets!

Upon Chief Massasoit's death his oldest son, Wamsutta, newly named Alexander, became great sachem of the Wampanoag nation. Shortly after celebrating the event, he received a summons to the court at Plymouth for "contriving mischief," an accusation that was false and humiliating to him. The matter was settled peacefully, but during this ordeal our leader became violently ill and within a handful of sleeps was dead. It was the unbearable heat of summer that killed him, the English said, but we are used to the deep warmth of Nippa'uus the sun. We believed he was poisoned.

So it was that Massasoit's second son, Metacomet, newly named

Philip, became great sachem of the Wampanoags. He carried the wound to the spirit of our people in his heart forever. Our lives hung in snares made by Englishmen and we could not escape. Metacomet was certain that all nations of red men living nearby must unite if we were to survive.

Once, not long ago, we needed few things. We moved from place to place with ease. We were comfortable in ourselves and in our lives. Now we have to account to the English or face trial in his court of laws. We have become strangers in this land of my grandfather's grandfather. Metacomet has also had to sign a treaty of submission. With darkness in our eyes we now watch Nippa'uus the sun rise each new day.

A Pilgrim's Story

Swansea Village, Plymouth Colony, June 1675

It is going from bad to worse with the Indians now. Why, last Thursday we were called to the meetinghouse to pray for peace, and while we were deep in prayer, savages skulked about our village, killed some of our grazing cattle, and, as if that were not enough, set fire to houses at the edge of town. One of our courageous boys shot and wounded an Indian whom we understand died shortly thereafter. But, to our horror, that boy and his father next day were murdered. We dispatched a messenger the fifty miles to Plymouth imploring for help, which, indeed, has come. Today more of our villagers have been tomahawked to death.

I am an old man now, one of the First Comers to Plymouth, and my days are numbered. I would like them to end peacefully but I fear this Indian uprising. God protect and preserve us.

I was born in England soon after the turn of the century. My family refused to worship according to King James's rules, as Church of England people did, knowing that only the Bible could instruct us in the way of the Lord. Thus we, and others of similar belief, chose to separate from the Church of England. For this we were not treated well and made a terrifying escape to Holland in 1608. There we lived for twelve years. My father was a weaver, but being not a Dutch citizen it was hard for him to earn a goodly wage in Holland.

My friends and I spoke Dutch with ease. It appeared that we children were losing our English ways, which displeased our families. But it was more than that: a treaty between Holland and Spain was soon to end. This could mean more misery for us if Holland and Spain went to war. With these concerns in mind, it was my family's decision, and that of others like us, to make a new life elsewhere. We chose the American wilderness as our destination.

Arrangements were made for two ships to make the voyage. The *Speedwell*, a small vessel which we boarded in Delftshaven, met the *Mayflower* with its English passengers, both "Saints" and "Strangers," in Southampton, England. On 5 August 1620, both ships set sail. Not far out

to sea the *Speedwell*'s seams opened and water came aboard. Twice we anxiously turned back to England for repairs. At last the *Mayflower*, alone, set sail for the New World in the season of foul weather, departing from Plymouth, England, 6 September 1620.

It was scarcely three months after we settled at New Plymouth that several red men came to our village in friendship. Among them was Chief Massasoit, great sachem of the Wampanoag people. In our weakened state, after that first death-filled winter, the Indians could have massacred us all, for we were only some fifty people, half being children. But it was God's will that we needed each other, especially for protection. In March of 1621 a peace treaty was signed by Governor Carver and Chief Massasoit.

It pleased us that the Indians had beaver skins to trade, which helped us pay our debt to the merchants who sponsored our settlement here. It pleased us, too, that we were able to occupy, without dispute, the abandoned cornfields we found here. Massasoit was accepting of our needs.

Chief Massasoit lived at Pokanoket on the Mount Hope Peninsula. Though he never became a Christian, he remained our very good friend. Squanto, our helpmate, lived among us for a few years until his death. Hubbamock and his family, our liaison with Massasoit, lived beside us. We were full of curiosity for one another.

It seems as though God has favored our endeavors for we are strong, now, in the number of us living along this coastal edge of New England, and we are without sickness, unlike the Indians. "The hand of God fell heavily upon them and they died in heapes."

But how difficult has been our task to civilize them. The fishermen and traders and explorers who came here in the last century reported to our monarch of a savage people living along the coast, smeared with red paint, mostly unclothed but for a breechcloth, and bedecked in strange feathers and ornaments. They worshiped not our Christian God. They spoke not English and read not and wrote not. They lived not in English houses and had not English gardens. It seemed as though they "but run over the grass as do also the foxes and wild beasts." They used what the land gave to them but owned it not, for they settled in no permanent way. Thus it was decreed that this New English land belonged to our sovereign, the king, for English folk, indeed, were the first civilized people to tame and improve this particular wilderness.

It is comforting to know that some of the Indians are taking to our religion because of the efforts of a few godly men. Pastor John Eliot is, in truth, a servant of the Lord. With great effort and much devotion he translated the Bible into the Massachusetts language and set up praying villages outside of Boston for teaching the savages to live in a godly way. Each village has a meetinghouse for Christian worship and English houses in rows with a broad street betwixt them for civilized living, with pastures and orchards and gardens to be cultivated. He has taught them to cut their hair and to dress in Englishmen's clothes as civilized folk do. Now there are fourteen praying villages hereabouts, some having as many as one hundred natives living there, with one of their own as pastor. There, too, are Praying Indians among the Wampanoags on Cape Cod and the nearby islands, thanks be to Almighty God.

Our countryside is dotted with towns and villages. Each village has a meetinghouse, a green for assemblage, and sturdy new houses clustered together for safety. At least one will serve as a garrison house in time of war.

Tension is growing, now, between ourselves and the Indians regarding this land. We need hay grounds and grazing meadows, garden plots and woodlots to support the many English people living here. Roger Williams of Providence Plantation says this land belongs to the Indians for they were its first occupants, but in signing our treaties they have

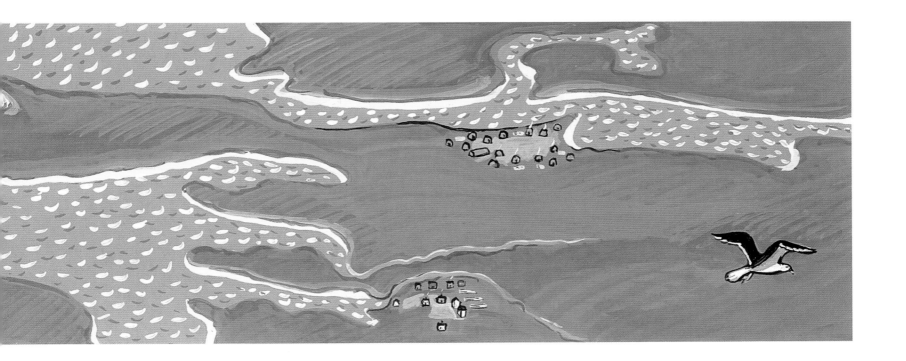

acknowledged that the land belongs to our king. How generous we have been in reserving the champion acreage of Mount Hope Peninsula for the Wampanoag people. That should satisfy their needs!

English Swansea and Indian Pokanoket sit side by side on this trembling earth. It seems as though there is a boundary betwixt them made of thorns. We love this country that gently rolls to the sea, with air so fresh and water so wholesome and a climate that invigorates us to work. We shall not be driven back to England!

I do believe the Indian Trouble began when our good friend, Chief Massasoit, died in 1662. His oldest boy, Wamsutta, then became leader of the Wampanoag people. At that time he was given a new name, Alexander, by the Plymouth court at his father's wish.

Soon after Alexander became great sachem of the Wampanoags, he was summoned to our court at Plymouth to explain his behavior. Had he been selling lands without our consent? Worse still, was he conspiring with the Narragansetts against us? We were much suspicious! When he failed to appear at court, Major Josiah Winslow and some militiamen were dispatched in search of him. They found Chief Alexander at his hunting house not far away. The weather was unbearably hot. Well I remember from the events that followed.

"The proud sachem fell into a rage of passion" for being accused of what he claimed were false rumors. After hours of questioning, it was decided that Chief Alexander's intentions were peaceful and he was excused, for the time being. Major Winslow invited the Indian party to his home to rest until the heat subsided. While there, Alexander took on a terrible sickness. A physician was brought from Plimoth Plantation to administer to his illness, but death came upon him shortly thereafter. It must have been the heat that caused Alexander to die. It could have been his terrible temper. Whatever the cause, tensions between the Wampanoags and ourselves became unbearable.

So it was that Metacomet, Massasoit's second son, became the next great sachem of the Wampanoags. He, too, was given an English name by the court at Plymouth. He was named Philip, and we have since called him King Philip. We are saddened that he is not our friend as was his father. In fact, we have found him to be like quicksand. We trust him not. He secretly desires for us to leave this New English land. His warriors now have scorched the edges of Swansea Village and put fire into our hearts, just as John Sassamon had predicted.

Poor John Sassamon! It was last winter that he was murdered, his body found under the ice with cuts and bruises about his head, his neck broken, his musket and hat on the ice nearby. It looked like an accident until the facts were uncovered.

The Indian, John Sassamon, born of the Massachusetts tribe, took quickly to our English ways and became a Christian. It was he who warned Plymouth Colony that King Philip would attack Swansea and warned us, also, that he would be murdered by King Philip should he be discovered. It was the Indian, Patuckson, who finally told us about witnessing the murder. Still, King Philip and his warriors claimed John Sassamon had died accidentally. The court at Plymouth, however, had no difficulty convicting three Indian men, and they were put to death. Justice was done.

A Wampanoag's Story

Yes, John Sassamon's body was found under the ice at Assawomsett Pond. He was a man back and forth in his loyalties. He lived sometimes in one of our settlements and sometimes at the Natick praying village. Not only was he a friend of Pastor John Eliot, and himself a Christian teacher, but was, at times, counselor and secretary of both Chiefs Wamsutta and Metacomet. We are sure that he warned Governor Winslow of our war preparations and so betrayed us.

Several months after John Sassamon's death, crafty Patuckson came forward to report to the English that our brother, Tobias, was guilty of murder. Tobias, at the time, was Metacomet's counselor. From high upon a hill, Patuckson claimed, he witnessed the event. But he was in debt to Tobias and would delight in his hanging. This fact was ignored by the English magistrates. Tobias was accused, along with his son and another man. All three pleaded innocent, yet all were put to death. Justice was not done.

It is the Towwa'keeswosh Moon, June 1675, by the white man's calendar. Yesterday a warrior was killed by a boy from Swansea. Today we sought revenge. Some braves murdered that boy and a man, then later killed more Englishmen and stuck their bloody hands and heads on poles. Let the English beware!

The war has begun, yet our nations have not united. Our friend, Chief Passaconway, once said, "You take heed how you quarrel with the English, for though you do them much mischief, yet assuredly you will all be destroyed and rooted off the earth if you do." Once we listened, but now we can no longer hear. We took heed how we quarreled with the English and we tried to share the land with them as all things share the earth, but in doing so we lost our freedom to tend to our needs, to honor the Spirit World, and to live, simply, as people.

As one of Metacomet's warriors I have painted myself fiercely and shaved my head for war. I have danced into a frenzy. My heart pounds into my bones. My musket is loaded. I will kill like a bear. I have no fear of death!

KING PHILIP'S WAR

A Pilgrim's Story

We are ready for war with the Indians but we would rather negotiate peace. There is so much to be done to subdue this wilderness of ours. We are most thankful that our New England colonies are united, all but that outcast group in Rhode Island. We will share strategies, men, and supplies, and we will be strong. If we catch King Philip on the Mount Hope Peninsula, the war will be over soon. If he escapes, then the countryside will be ignited by the uprising. God protect and preserve us.

A Wampanoag's Story

We will take back this land, or die. The English are cumbersome in warfare. They prefer to fight in lines on open battlefields. We easily slip through the woods in darkness, across the river to the swamp where our footsteps vanish . . . then away! We hear that the Narragansetts have signed a treaty of submission with the English. It will not last, for their chief is keen like a fox. We have attacked Rehoboth and Taunton. We have torched Middleborough and Dartmouth. The countryside burns! We will be free!

A Pilgrim's Story

The war now has moved inland as though swept by a witch's broom scattering cinders this way and that. In August, Brookfield was attacked, then Lancaster; Deerfield and Squakeag in September; Hadley and Springfield early in October, then Hatfield. Our people are frightened, their houses burned, the mills destroyed. We have no ground corn for our soldiers' bread. Our crops are ravaged, our families broken by death and war. We thought we were fighting only the Wampanoags, but we now are fighting the treacherous Nipmucks, too.

A Wampanoag's Story

Metacomet has run beyond Nipmuck country to the land of the warring Mohawks, but they remain his enemy. He must return as we fight on, burning and killing as we go. We make soft noises within a village at the first light of the day and kill whatever stirs. We take women and children as captives and hope to sell them for ransom. But we are low on food. Our untended harvest is being destroyed. Our warriors, too, are caught and killed. Diseases, again, spread among us. The English have put many of our praying people on Deer Island in Boston Harbor and on islands elsewhere without food or shelter. We burn the Englishmen's Black Book!

A Pilgrim's Story

It is mid-December 1675, and bitter cold. We now fear the Narragansetts for they do not honor our treaty. They do not return fugitive red men to Boston. Governor Winslow, now commander of the army, plans to attack Narragansett country. Captain Benjamin Church, his aide, is ready for war, but our troops are slow to arrive at the garrison house. Supplies, too, are low. We have captured some Narragansetts, including Indian Peter, who promises to take us to the Great Swamp, the hiding place of his people. Joining our forces are friendly Mohegans and Pequots. They are our best informers.

A Wampanoag's Story

Narragansett warriors now join us in this great uprising. Word, however, had reached us of a terrible massacre of the Narragansett people. On an island deep in the Great Swamp they had built a village of many, many wigwams to shelter themselves and their food. There they felt safe. But one of their own betrayed them. Peter led the English across the swamp ice to the only opening in their fortress. The English attacked and soon the sky blazed with fire from their burning wigwams. Hundreds of Narragansett people perished that night. Those who escaped fled into the frozen darkness.

A Pilgrim's Story

Morale is low. Soldiers are deserting. In February, Pastor Rowlandson's wife and children were taken captive, and houses were burned in Medfield and Mendon. More villages were attacked in March. Eleven people were killed at Plymouth, the garrison house was burned, and Roger Williams's house and others were destroyed in Providence. Through early spring, war burst out in settlements from the valley of the Connecticut River to villages encircling Boston. Our people are filled with fear! But Captain William Turner's success at the falls of Peskeomscut on May 19 gives us hope.

A Wampanoag's Story

Metacomet will not negotiate peace. Those wishing to live now surrender. We are divided among ourselves, and we are so hungry! But it is the Namassackee'wush Moon, time to catch fish. Thank you Great Spirit for making it so! Then early one morning, as salmon swam up river at Peskeomscut, the English surprised us in attack. Whole families died in the slaughter, or were drowned. How sickened we are by our great loss.

Mohawks join in the fight against us. Sachems are being captured and executed. Our ammunition is low, but we fight on.

A Pilgrim's Story

It is summer and we are full of hope. Squaw Sachem Awashonks and her band of Wampanoags have surrendered. Indian informers tell us that King Philip is returning to the Mount Hope Peninsula, his homeland. We will catch him there. On July 3, a goodly number of Indians were killed at Warwick. July 27, many more surrendered at Boston. They will be hanged or sold into slavery or used here as servants. On August 1, we captured King Philip's wife and small son. We will sell them as slaves. It is 1676 in the year of Our Lord.

A Wampanoag's Story

Among those of our people who have surrendered are traitors. They have become the eyes and the ears of the English, telling them how we fight and where we hide. So it happened that a Wampanoag led the English to Metacomet's wigwam. Our great sachem escaped into the Mirey Swamp. There he was shot and his body quartered to the cheers of Englishmen. But his spirit was then set free.

I have been captured and will be hanged on Boston Common. I, too, am prepared to die, for I know that my spirit will live in a happier place, through happier days, again with my people.

GLOSSARY

BLACK BOOK—the Bible

BREECHCLOTH—a long, often foot-wide piece of animal skin worn by Native American men to cover their loins

DISEASES (brought to the New World by European explorers, traders, and settlers)—smallpox, chicken pox, measles, influenza, hepatitis

FIRST COMERS—earliest settlers of Plimoth Plantation, Mayflower passengers

GARRISON HOUSE—a safe house used by the townspeople in time of war, fortified with soldiers and ammunition, and a food supply

GREAT SACHEM—chief over the many subtribes (bands) that make up a nation or federation; the Wampanoag nation, the Nipmuck nation, the Narragansett nation

GREAT SEA—Atlantic Ocean

GREAT SPIRIT (KIEHTAN)—believed by the Wampanoags to be the creator, residing in the Southwest

MAGISTRATE—someone who can enforce the law, a judge

MASSACHUSETTS LANGUAGE—a dialect of the Algonquian language

MEDICINE MAN—a Native American believed to have spiritual powers

MILITIAMEN—armed citizens

MISHOON—a dugout canoe, hollowed from a chestnut or pine log

MOONS—months

PALISADE—a tall fence made of branchless trees, serving as a protective wall

PARCHMENT—a paperlike material made of goatskin or sheepskin

SACHEM—chief of a band, or subtribe, of a Native American nation; the Patuxets, Sakonnets, Pocassets, Mashpees, and Pokanokets were all subtribes of the Wampanoag nation, each with its own sachem

SAGAMORE—a minor Algonquian Indian chief

"SAINTS" AND "STRANGERS"—Pilgrims and other English

SAMP—cornmeal porridge

SECRETARY—confidential adviser

SHOOTING STICKS—guns

SPIRIT WORLD—the world of unseen beings, believed to be everywhere, in everything

TRUCKING CLOTH—cloth used for trade, especially dark blue and dark red woolen blanket material

WAMPUM—small beads made from the purple and white parts of quahog shells

LIST OF CHARACTERS

ALEXANDER—see Wamsutta

BENJAMIN CHURCH—of Plymouth Colony, captain in the militia, famous for his diary of King Philip's War

CORBITANT—sachem of the Pocasset band of Wampanoags at the time the Pilgrims were settling Plimoth Plantation

HUBBAMOCK—a Pokanoket (Wampanoag) member of Massasoit's tribal council, liaison between the Pilgrims and Massasoit, who lived with his family beside Plimoth Plantation

JOHN CARVER—a Mayflower passenger and first governor of Plimoth Plantation

JOHN ELIOT—Puritan clergyman of Massachusetts Bay Colony, a teacher of Christianity to the Native Americans who translated the Bible into the Massachusetts language

JOHN SASSAMON—Native American born of the Massachusetts who became a Praying Indian, friend of both Pilgrims and Wampanoag, whose mysterious death sparked King Philip's War

JOSIAH WINSLOW—son of Edward Winslow, a Mayflower passenger. He was major in the Plymouth Colony army, then commander in chief; governor of Plymouth Colony from 1673–1680

MASSASOIT (THE GREAT ONE)—great sachem of the Wampanoag nation at the time the Pilgrims landed in 1620 until his death in 1662, and sachem of the Pokanokets; father of Wamsutta (Alexander), Metacomet (Philip), another son named Sunconewhew, and a daughter, Amie

METACOMET (PHILIP)—second son of Massasoit and great sachem of the Wampanoag nation from approximately 1662 until his death in the war bearing his name, King Philip's War, August 12, 1676

PASSACONWAY—great sachem of the Pennacook nation and sachem of the Patucket band of the Pennacooks

PHILIP (KING PHILIP)—see Metacomet

ROGER WILLIAMS—Puritan clergyman, founder of Rhode Island, creator of a dictionary for the Narragansetts

SAMOSET—believed to have been an Abanaki sagamore, who was first to greet the Pilgrims in March 1621

SQUANTO—a Patuxet (Wampanoag), once captive on an Englishman's ship, helpmate and friend of the Pilgrims who lived at Plimoth Plantation

WAMSUTTA (ALEXANDER)—Massasoit's oldest son, and, until his untimely death, great sachem of the Wampanoag nation

WILLIAM TURNER—a captain in King Philip's War, resident of Massachusetts Bay Colony, leader of the successful English attack at Peskeomscut

SELECTED SOURCE MATERIAL USED IN THIS TEXT

Axtell, James. *The European and the Indian: Essays in the Ethnohistory of Colonial North America*. New York: Oxford University Press, 1981.

Bonfanti, Leo. *Biographies and Legends of the New England Indians*. Vols. 1–4. Mass.: Pride Publications, 1968-1974.

Bourne, Russell. *The Red King's Rebellion: Racial Politics in New England, 1675–1678*. New York: Atheneum, 1990.

Bradford, William. *Of Plimoth Plantation 1620–1647*. New York: Random House Inc., 1981.

Church, Colonel Benjamin. *Diary of King Philip's War*. Mass.: Little Compton Historical Society, 1975.

Cronon, William. *Changes in the Land: Indians, Colonists, and the Ecology of New England*. New York: McGraw-Hill, 1983.

Gill, Crispin. *Mayflower Remembered*. New York: Taplinger Publishing Co., 1970.

Hubbard, William. *The History of the Indian Wars in New England from the First Settlement to the Termination of the War with King Philip*. 1677. Samuel G. Drake edition, vol. 1. Roxbury, Mass., 1865.

Jennings, Frances, *The Invasion of America: Indians, Colonialism, and the Cant of Conquest*. Chapel Hill: University of North Carolina Press, 1975.

Leach, Douglas Edward. *Flintlock and Tomahawk: New England in King Philip's War*. New York: Norton, 1953.

Mather, Increase. *The History of King Philip's War*. 1676. Samuel G. Drake edition. Boston, 1862.

Mourt's Relation. *The Journal of the Pilgrims at Plymouth, in New England, in 1620*. 1622. Reprint, New York: Corinth Books, 1963.

Salisbury, Neal. *Manitou and Providence: Indians, Europeans, and the Making of New England 1500-1643*. New York: Oxford University Press, 1982.

Simmons, William S. *The Spirit of New England Tribes: Indian History and Folklore, 1620–1984*. Hanover and London: University Press of New England, 1986.

Vaughan, Alden T. *New England Frontier: Puritans and Indians 1620–1675*. Boston: Little, Brown and Co., 1965.

Whipple, Chandler. *First Encounter: The Indian and the White Man in New England*. Mass.: The Berkshire Traveller Press, 1972.

Wilbur, C. Keith. *The New England Indians*. Conn.: The Globe Pequot Press, 1978.

Williams, Roger. *A Key into the Language of America*. 1643. Reprint, edited by John J. Teunissen and Evelyn J. Hinz. Detroit: Wayne State University Press, 1973.

Willison, George F. *Saints and Strangers*. New York: Reynal and Hitchcock, 1945.

Winslow, Ola Elizabeth. *John Eliot, Apostle to the Indians*. Boston: Houghton Mifflin Co., 1968.

Wood, William. *New England's Prospect*. London, 1634. Edited by Alden T. Vaughan. Cambridge: University of Massachusetts Press, 1977.

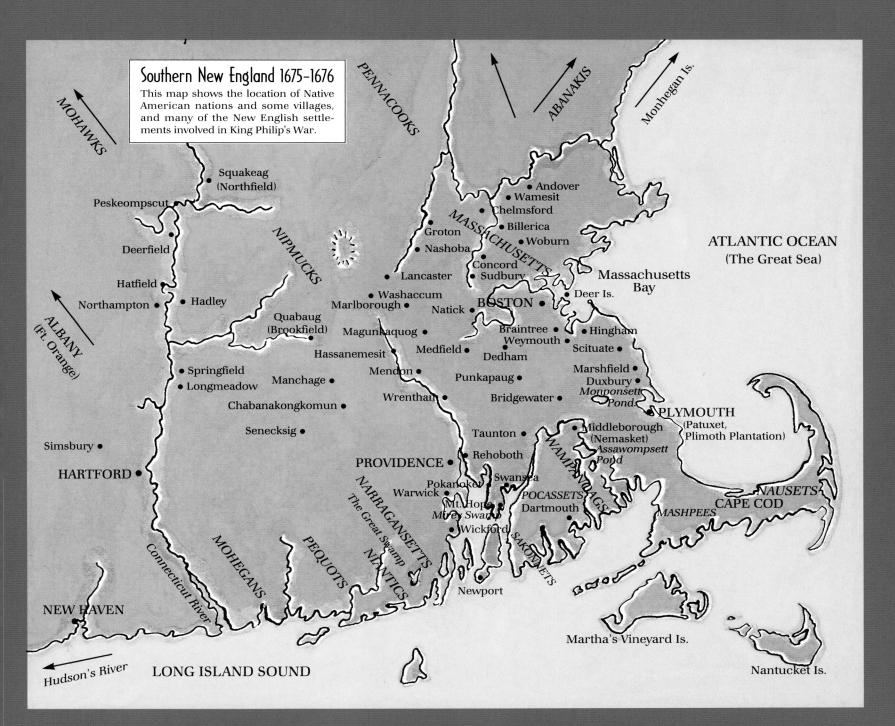

Southern New England 1675–1676

This map shows the location of Native American nations and some villages, and many of the New English settlements involved in King Philip's War.

MOHAWKS

PENNACOOKS

ABANAKIS

Monhegan Is.

Squakeag
(Northfield)

Peskeompscut

Andover
Wamesit
Chelmsford
Billerica
Groton
Woburn
Nashoba

MASSACHUSETTS

Deerfield

NIPMUCKS

Hatfield
Northampton
Hadley

ALBANY
(Ft. Orange)

Quabaug
(Brookfield)

Concord
Lancaster
Sudbury

Washaccum
Marlborough
Natick

BOSTON

Deer Is.

Massachusetts
Bay

ATLANTIC OCEAN
(The Great Sea)

Magunkaquog
Hassanemesit

Medfield

Braintree
Weymouth
Dedham

Hingham
Scituate

Springfield
Longmeadow
Manchage

Mendon

Punkapaug

Marshfield
Duxbury
Monponsett
Pond

Chabanakongkomun

Wrentham

Bridgewater

PLYMOUTH
(Patuxet,
Plimoth Plantation)

Senecksig

Taunton

Middleborough
(Nemasket)
Assawompsett
Pond

WAMPANOAGS

Simsbury

HARTFORD

PROVIDENCE

Rehoboth

Warwick
Pokanoket
Swansea

POCASSETS

Dartmouth

NAUSETS
CAPE COD

MASHPEES

NARRAGANSETTS
The Great Swamp

Mt. Hope
Mirey Swamp
Wickford

SAKONNETS

MOHEGANS

PEQUOTS

NIANTICS

Newport

NEW HAVEN

Connecticut River

Martha's Vineyard Is.

Hudson's River

LONG ISLAND SOUND

Nantucket Is.